DECORATIVE DOGS

A COLOURFUL FURRY ADVENTURE

Copyright © 2016 Christopher Mark Stokes

First edition published in 2016

All colouring images herein have been illustrated by the artist and therefore may not be reproduced without the owner's permission.

Conditions of Sale

This book is sold subject to the condition that it shall not, by the way of trade or otherwise be lent, resold, hired out or otherwise circulated without the artists prior written consent in any form of binding or cover than which it is published.

www.christophermarkstokes.yolasite.com

DECORATIVE DOGS

A COLOURFUL FURRY ADVENTURE

PUG

SHAR-PEI

GERMAN SHEPHERD

AFGHAN HOUND

GREAT DANE

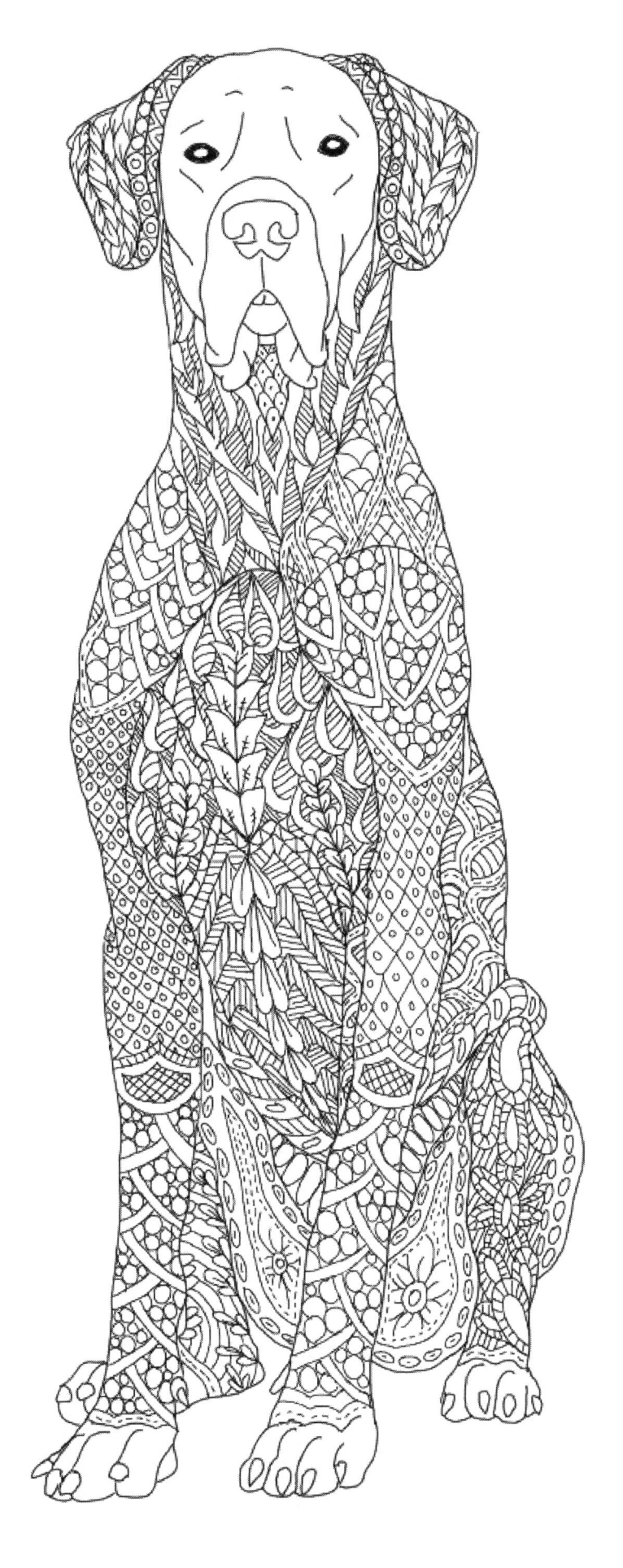

NEWFOUNDLAND

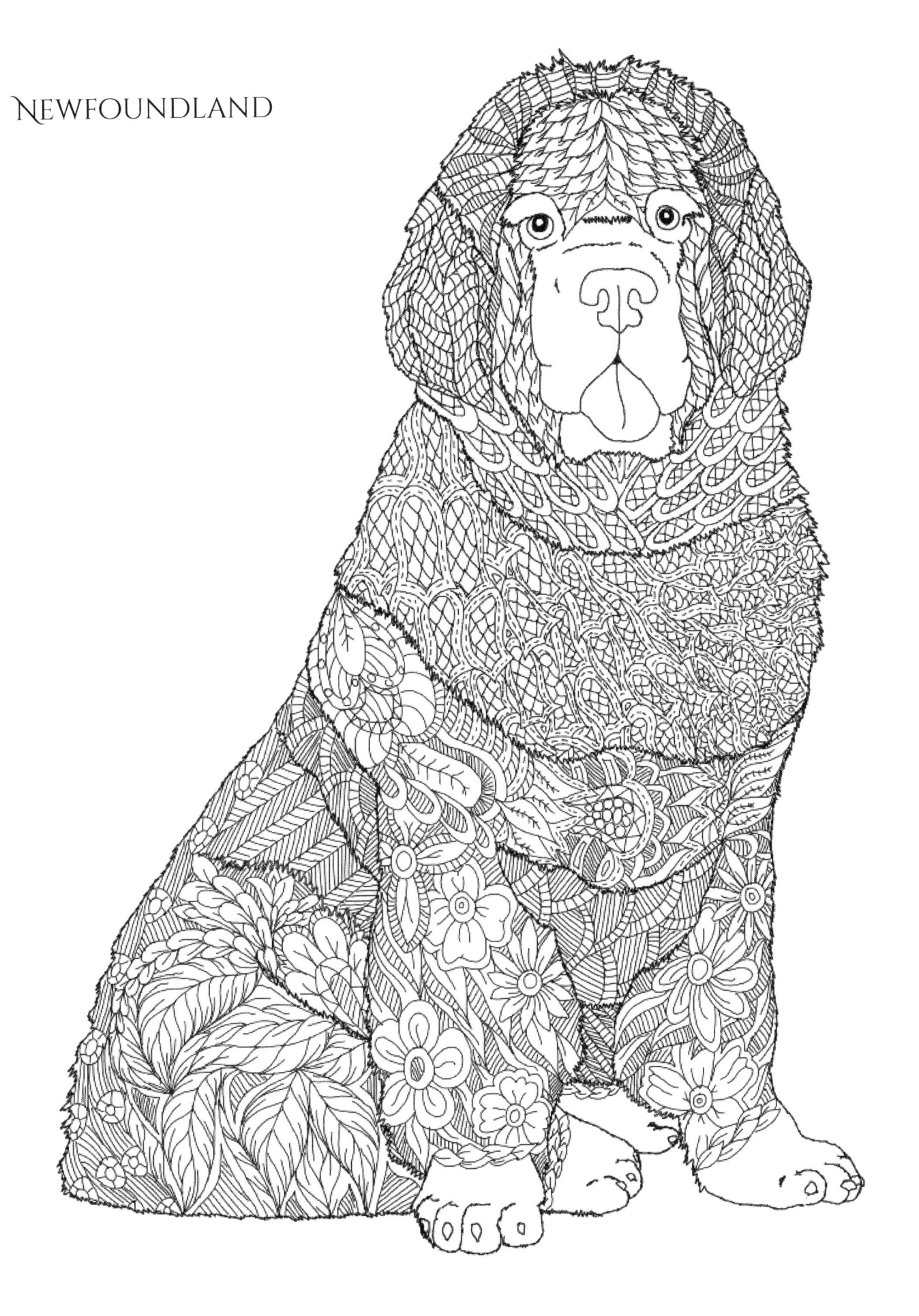

CHIHUAHUA

ENGLISH BULLDOG

POODLE

AKITA

CORGI

BASSET HOUND

GREY HOUND

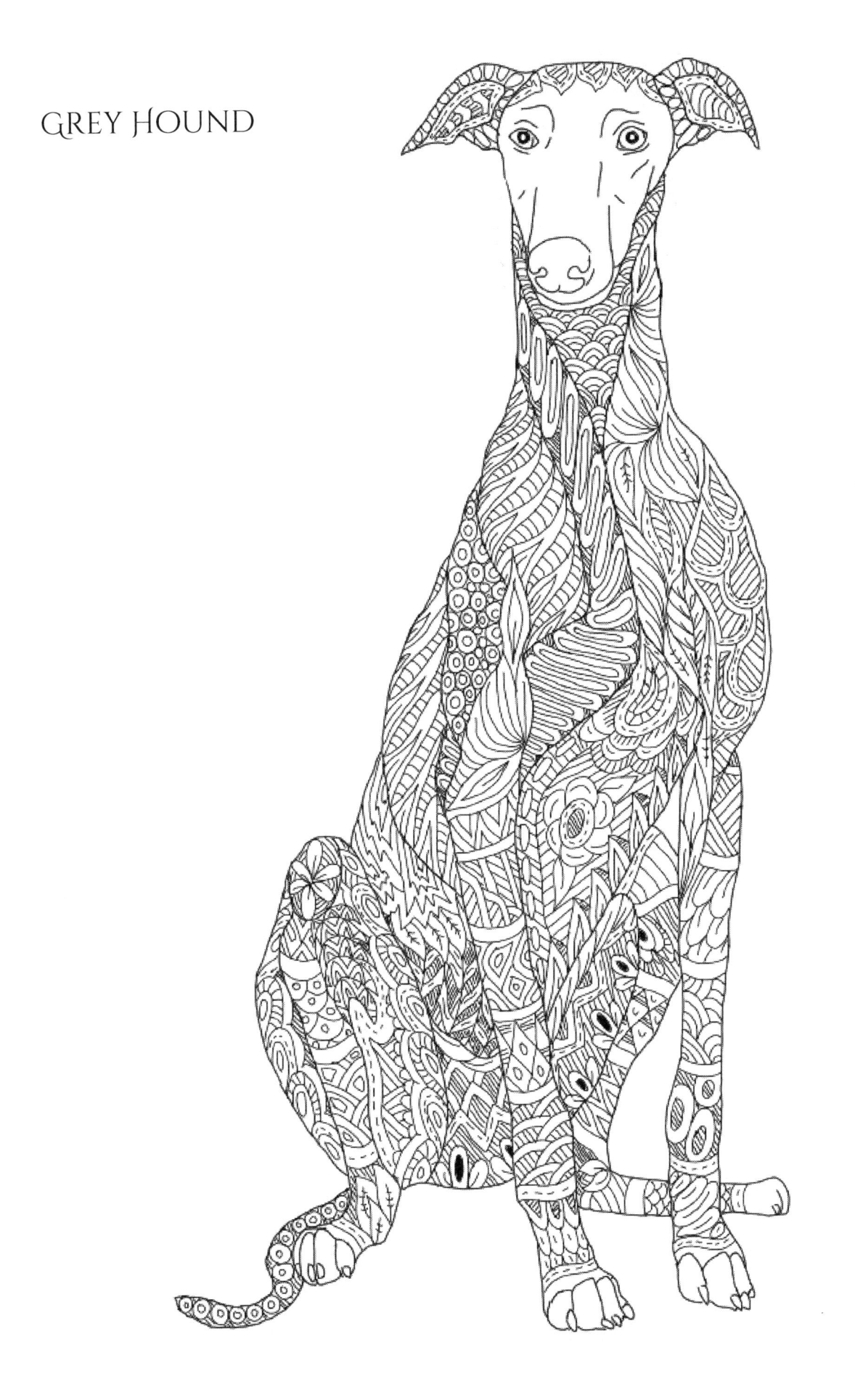

SHETLAND
SHEEPDOG

BICHON FRISE

SHIH TZU

DACHSHUND

LABRADOR

YORKSHIRE
TERRIER

BEAGLE

SAINT
BERNARD

SCHNAUZER

CHOW CHOW

JACK RUSSELL

BOXER

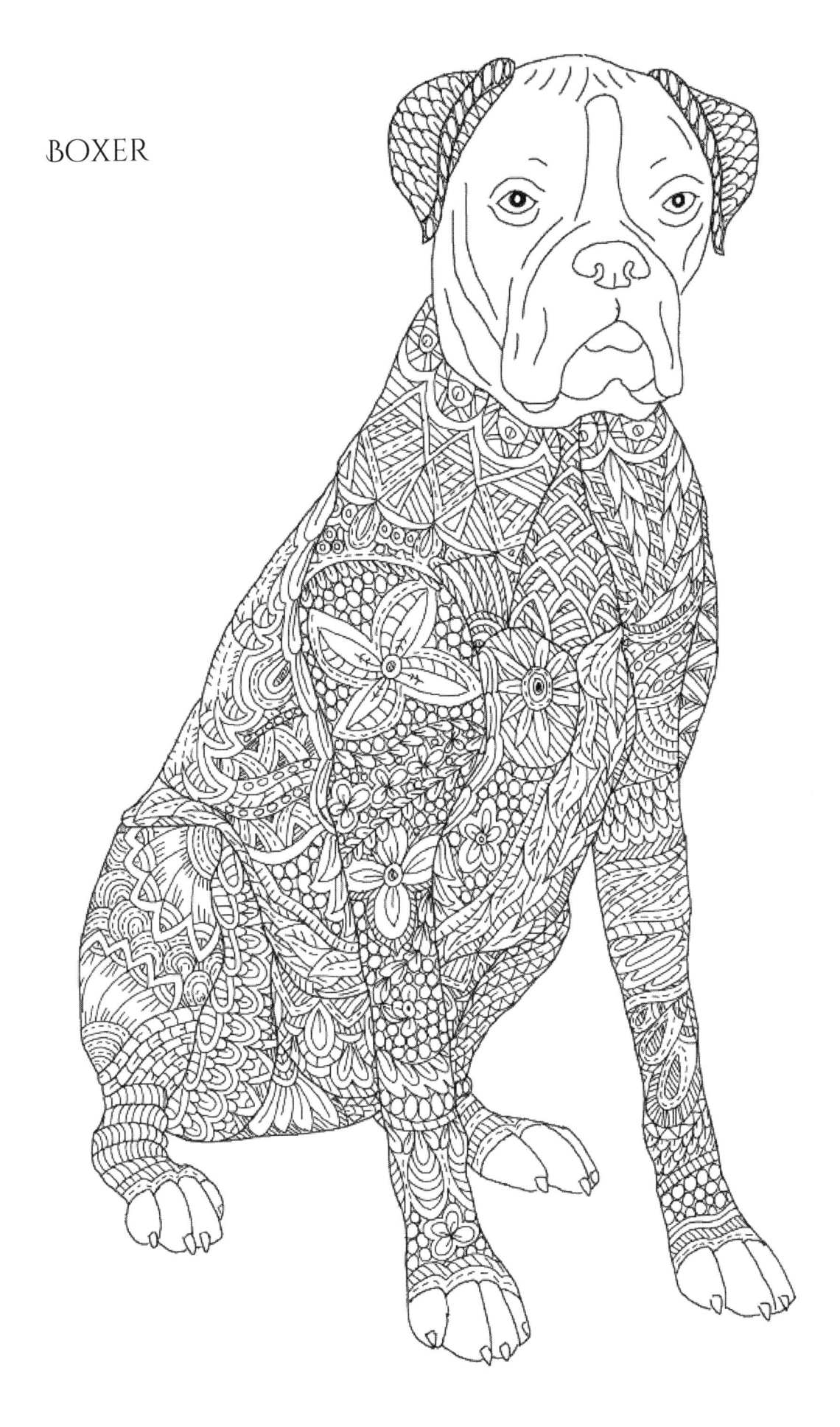

BULLMASTIFF

TRY IT YOURSELF:

Unleash your creativeness upon these canine outlines and add some details of your very own; or, simply colour them in and bring the dogs to life in whatever way your artistic side desires.

DECORATIVE DOGS

A COLOURFUL FURRY ADVENTURE

About the Artist

Christopher Mark Stokes was born on 8th January, and currently resides in Walsall in the West Midlands within the United Kingdom.
Already Christopher Mark Stokes has seen some of his books become bestsellers in various amazon categories, and with the constant support of his family he has written two novels; one in the fantasy genre and one in horror. Alongside these he has also written novellas and numerous short stories.

Christopher has also used his passion for art in order to create a plethora of illustrated children's books aimed at a variety of age groups; from two year old's to twelve year old's.

Christopher loves all things in relation to science fiction, fantasy and horror. Inspirations for his work are authors such as George R.R Martin, J.R.R Tolkien, Stephen King, Clive Barker and children's author Roald Dahl. He is also inspired by illustrator Quentin Blake.

ALSO AVAILABLE:

Christopher Mark Stokes

Natures Creatures
a colourful animal adventure

Printed in Great Britain
by Amazon